KETOGENIC DIET

SIDE DISHES COOKBOOK

Felicity Flinn

Table of Contents

SIDE DISHES 7

Keto Spaghetti Squash Casserole 8

Garlicky Greens Bean Stir Fry.......................................10

Roasted Asparagus w/ Garlic, Lemon, & Parmesan....13

Fluffy Low-Carb Mashed Cauliflower with Celery Root (Keto)... 15

Zucchini & Sweet Potato Latkes 18

Grilling Zucchini 20

Oven-Fried Parmesan Zucchini Rounds......................22

Keto Egg Fast Fettuccini Alfredo 24

Grilled Eggplant Salad...26

Pan-Roasted Radishes (Low-Carb & Gluten-Free) 29

Four Ingredient Sugar-Free Cranberry Sauce 31

Pico de Gallo 33

Low-Carb Onion Rings 34

Roasted Spicy Garlic Eggplant Slices 36

3

Roasted Baby Eggplant... 38

Crispy Fried Eggplant Rounds With Parmesan Cheese and Marinara Sauce... 40

Artichoke with Herbed Mayonnaise 43

Spicy Stir-Fried Sugar Snap Peas.................................45

Roasted Cabbage Wedges with Onion Dijon Sauce.....47

Roasted Salt & Pepper Radish Chips 49

Baked Artichoke Hearts Au Gratin 51

Oven Roasted Basil Parmesan Tomatoes 54

Mashed Cauliflower with Parmesan & Chives.............56

Garlic Mashed Cauliflower 58

Goat Cheese Cauliflower Bake Recipe 59

Cauliflower Cheesy Alla Vodka Casserole....................62

Feta Stuffing and Low-Carb Pumpkin Bread 64

Keto Spicy Sausage and Cheddar Stuffing.................. 66

Gluten-Free Stuffing & Low-Carb 69

Low-Carb Tortillas.. 71

Two Mins Low-Carb English Muffin............................73

Cheesy Garlic Bread Muffins............................75

Braided Garlic Breadsticks 78

Bread and dried Sun Tomato – Low-Carb...................81

Low-Carb Cranberry Relish (Keto) 84

Parmesan Garlic Roasted Mushrooms 86

Creamy Cauliflower Mash with Kale (Low-Carb
Colcannon)...88

Parmesan Rosti & Low-Carb Celeriac Bacon..............90

Garlic Butter Sautéed Spinach 92

Low-Carb Coconut Creamed Spinach.........................94

Buttery Bacon Brussels Sprouts..................................96

Stir-Fried Bok Choy with Soy Butter & Sauce 98

Low-Carb Cheesy Brussels Sprouts Gratin................100

Low-Carb Creamy Greek Zucchini Patties.................102

Spaghetti Squash with Garlic and Parsley 104

Spaghetti Squash with Garlic, Bacon & Parmesan....106

THANK YOU...109

SIDE DISHES

Keto Spaghetti Squash Casserole

(Ready in about 35 mins |Serving 6| Difficulty: Easy)

Per serving: Kcal 168, Fat:13g, Net Carbs:4g Protein:8g

Ingredients

- Spaghetti squash cooked 2 cups

- Egg 1

- Herbs de Provence 1 tsp

- Onion & chive cream flavored cheese 8 oz

- Pinch of salt

- Mozzarella cheese 1 cup

Instructions

1. Oven preheated to 350.
2. Liquid the baking spray in a baking dish. Place the baked spaghetti vegetables in the dish.
3. In a quick processor, add the milk, cream cheese, herbs & salt. Mix until smooth. Pour it over the vegetable spaghetti.
4. Scatter of cheese over it. Bake until white, for thirty to forty mins.

Garlicky Green Beans Stir Fry

(Ready in about 25 mins |Serving 4| Difficulty: Easy)

Per serving: Cal 171, Fat:7g, Net Carbs:8.5g Protein:6g

Ingredients

- Fresh green beans 1 lb.

- Peanut oil 2 t

- Chopped garlic 2 t

- Yellow onion 1/2 small

- Salt 1/4 tsp

- oyster sauce 2 t

Instructions

1. Cut green beans on both sides.
2. Slice the green beans into 2-inch pieces, wash and spin dry with paper towels in the salad spinner (affiliate link). (Beans bought do not need to wash.)
3. Heat the wok or a large frying pan over high heat for 1-2 minutes, before your hand is too hot to stay over it.
4. Add the oil and boil for around 30 seconds, then add the slivers of garlic and onion, and simmer for 20-30 seconds, stirring the entire time.
5. Connect beans and salt and cook, stirring many times, for around 2 minutes.
6. Then add hot, cover wok, and let steam beans for five minutes. (I tested once to see if the pan appeared dry and applied around 1 tsp. more water.)

7. Uncover the pan and apply the oyster sauce, then cook for another 2 minutes, stirring so that all the beans are completely coated with the sauce.

8. When they're finished, beans can always be slightly crisp. Serve wet.

9. This can be stored for a day or two in the refrigerator and reheated in the oven, although you'll still have a little leftover.

Roasted Asparagus with Garlic, Lemon, & Parmesan

(Ready in about 15 mins |Serving 4| Difficulty: Easy)

Per serving: Cal 173, Fat:4g, Net Carbs:6g Protein:7g

Ingredients

- Asparagus 1 bunch

- Olive oil 3-4 tbsp

- Ground black pepper & Kosher salt

- Chopped garlic 2 cloves

- Grated Parmesan cheese 3 tbsp

- Juice of lemon 1/2

Instructions

1. Oven preheated to 425 ºc.
2. Clean the garden asparagus & cut each stalk's bottom inch, get rid of the stiff, fibrous portion. It is a simple way to say when to cut to curve 1 asparagus stalk to the edge until it snaps away. Place it beside the remaining of the garden asparagus and split both of them to about the same weight.
3. Pat the garden asparagus to dry and scatter over a cookie sheet in a thin layer. Silt only with olive oil, then gently spray with flake salt & black pepper (fresh). Grant the asparagus a toss in the olive oil and seasoning to cover it uniformly, after which bake it in the oven for 8-10 mins, depending on size, until tender.
4. Take it from the oven & brush with garlic, Parmesan cheese, & lemon juice. Before eating, add another toss.

Fluffy Low-Carb Mashed Cauliflower with Celery Root (Keto)

(Ready in about 25 mins |Serving 6| Difficulty: Easy)

Per serving: Kcal 158, Fat:9g, Net Carbs:3g Protein:2g

Ingredients

- Cauliflower florets 1 pound

- Celeriac cubed & peeled 1 small

- Chopped garlic clove 1 large

- Heavy cream 1/3 cup

- Stick butter 1/2

- Salt & pepper

- Variations

- Add buttermilk for heavy cream

- Sub 1 lemon zest

- Top it with green onion

- Top it with minced parsley

- Top it with "bacon."

- Top it with fine cheddar

Instructions

1. **Celeriac:** Strip off the knob celery top & bottom. Then with a small knife & operating from top to bottom, cut the root as though you were about to supreme a grapefruit. Slice the knob celery into 1/2-inch slices, put the sliced garlic in a pot & cover with water. Carry the knob celery to a simmer & cook until soft, then pierce it quickly with a fork.

2. **Cauliflower:** Slice the cauliflower onto florets & put it in a bowl of microwavable. Apply two tbsp of water, cover & bake for 5 to 8 mins at high

intensity or once the cauliflower is soft & pierced with such a fork.

3. **Puree:** put the cauliflower & knob celery (with garlic) in a mixing bowl & pulse the bits to separate. Apply the puree & whipping cream until smooth. Stir in butter, then blend properly. Garnish with pepper & salt. Then blend in the mash the chives.

Zucchini & Sweet Potato Latkes

(Ready in about 40 mins |Serving 1| Difficulty: Easy)

Per serving: Cal 122, Fat:9g, Net Carbs:6.25g Protein:3g

Ingredients

- Shredded zucchini 1 cup

- Shredded sweet potato 1 cup

- Beaten egg 1

- Coconut flour 1 tbsp

- Garlic powder 1/2 tsp

- Ground cumin 1/4 tsp

- Dried parsley 1/2 tsp

- Salt & pepper to taste

- Clarified butter 1 tbsp

- Extra virgin olive oil 1 tbsp

Instructions

1. In a med dish, add the courgette, sweet potato & egg.

2. Mix the coconut flour as well as the spices in a shallow bowl. Apply the courgette combination to the dry ingredients and blend until thoroughly mixed.

3. Heat the butter in a med non-stick skillet & the olive oil. Split the combination into 4 equal parts & fall into the saucepan. Push it down using a fork until a layer is shaped 1/2 inch thick. Cook until crispy & golden on med heat, then turn safely & bake the different side. Drop and drain onto a tray lined with tissue paper.

4. Top with an extra flake Salt. Serve warm

Grilling Zucchini

(Ready in about 25 mins |Serving 1| Difficulty: Easy)

Per serving: Cal 196, Fat:16g, Net Carbs:3.9g Protein:2g

Ingredients

- Two sliced zucchinis 10 to 12 inch long

- Vinaigrette salad 1/2 cup

- Garlic powder 1 tsp

Instructions

1. Break the courgette into pieces to guarantee the pieces are similar in thickness.

2. Mix your option of salad dressing, including garlic powder & dried herbs, if available.

3. Place the courgette pieces into the Ziploc container, add in the marinade and let the courgette marinate in the refrigerator for 4 hours or longer, or as long as needed for the entire day.

4. Drain the courgette into a colander put inside the sink until you are about to serve.

5. Heat it grills to med-high to roast courgette. If needed, you should spray your grill using a non-stick spray. However, the marinade does have plenty of oil, so you don't need it anyway.

6. Place the courgette diagonally on the grill pan, holding a spray bottle ready to tame any flames in the marinade that could rise from the grease.

7. Look for grill marks after 3-4 mins & if you see them move courgette heading the other way around. Cook 3 to 4 mins after you have gone spinning.

8. Switch the zucchini onto the other side & roast for some more mins or before the courgette starts to melt, with the exterior somewhat brown.

9. Top with pepper & salt fresh in the ground and serve warm.

Oven-Fried Parmesan Zucchini Rounds

(Ready in about 30 mins |Serving 12| Difficulty: Easy)

Per serving: kcal 71, Fat:4g, Net Carbs:3g Protein:6g

Ingredients

- 3 large zucchini, sliced (6 cups sliced rounds)

- 1 whole egg

- 1 egg white

- 1 1/2cups parmesan cheese, grated

- 1/4 cup fresh parsley, chopped

- 1/2 teaspoon garlic powder

- Olive oil cooking spray

Instructions

1. Oven preheated to 425oC.
2. Spray cookie sheets with baking Spray

3. Hit the egg white, set aside in a small bowl.
4. Put the Parmesan, parsley, and garlic powder in a different bowl and stir well.
5. Dip the Courgette in the mixture of the eggs, then in Parmesan, put it on the cookie sheet.
6. Don't cross courgettes on cookie dish.
7. Cook for ten mins, then turn them over and cook for ten mins, or until it becomes golden brown.

Keto Egg Fast Fettuccini Alfredo

(Ready in about 20 mins |Serving 1| Difficulty: Easy)

Per serving: kcal 491, Fat:47g, Net Carbs:2g Protein:19g

Ingredients

For the pasta:

- Eggs 2

- Cream cheese 1 oz

- Pinch salt

- Pinch of garlic powder

- Black pepper 1/8 tsp

For the sauce:

- Mascarpone cheese 1 oz

- Grated parmesan cheese 1 tbsp

- Butter 1 Tbsp

Instructions

For pasta:

1. In a grinder, add your eggs, cheese, cream, spice, garlic powder & pepper. Put into an 8 x 8 tray greased with butter. Bake eight minutes at 324 or before you just set. Remove& allow it to cool for five mins. Use a spatula to release the "pasta" sheet from the pan nicely. Turn it over and slice all into one/eight-inch thick pieces with a fine knife. Unroll softly, then put back.

For the sauce:

1. In a shallow cup, add the mascarpone, the parmesan cheese, and butter. 30 Second microwave on big. Click. Then click. Microwave another 30 seconds on big. Whisk until smooth again (this will take a minute since the sauce may be scattered-keep whisking, and it will come back together.) Add the pasta to the hot sauce and mix gently. Serve directly with freshly ground black pepper.

Grilled Eggplant Salad

(Ready in about 42 mins |Serving 6| Difficulty: Easy)

Per serving: Cal 183, Fat:10g, Net Carbs:23g Protein:4.3g

Ingredients:

- Thin Asian Eggplants 6

- Olive oil 1T to brush eggplants

- Fresh-& salty ground black pepper to season eggplants

- Grape tomatoes 1 cup

- Crumbled Feta 1/2 cup

Dressing ingredients:

- Fresh basil leaves 2/3 cup

- parsley leaves 1/3 cup

- large sliced garlic cloves 2

- Dijon mustard 1 t

- capers 3 t

- lemon juice 2 t

- additional-virgin olive oil 1/4 cup

Instructions

1. Heat up until med-high to BBQ.
2. Clean the aubergine if possible, then cut two ends. Cut the aubergine lengthwise, brown on both sides with olive oil, then top with salt & pepper upon its cut side
3. Put the cut side aubergine on your plate, then cook until you see some nice grill grates (about 5 to 7 mins).
4. Turn aubergine & cook for about five mins on the other hand, or until the aubergine is softened & very well browned.
5. Take the aubergine off from the cutting board & let It cool. Cut the tomatoes(grape) in half to make the beautiful dressing as the aubergine cool down.

6. Clean and turn as needed, dry out the basil & parsley leaves.
7. Choose the garlic cloves, then use a food processor with a steel blade to slice basil, peters, & ginger.
8. Apply the Dijon, capers, as well as lemon juice, then mix until the ingredients combine well; Now add the olive oil & stir it for thirty seconds.
9. Split it into pieces about one inch across, if the aubergine is treatable sufficiently.
10. Mix the aubergine & tomato halves nicely in a bowl and blend to coat the ingredients in a bread dressing (around 1/4 cup). For just another moment, save the remainder of dressing; too many things are perfect.
11. Apply a crumbled Feta & enjoy it.

Pan-Roasted Radishes (Low-Carb & Gluten-Free)

(Ready in about 60 mins | Serving 2| Difficulty: Easy)

Per serving: kcal 122, Fat:12g, Net Carbs:2.75g Protein:1g

Ingredients

- Quartered radishes 2 cups

- Butter 2 tbsp

- Lemon zest 1 tbsp

- Chopped chives 1 tbsp

- Pepper & salt to taste

Instructions

1. Melt the butter on a big, sauté pan. Apply the radishes, turn them down to protect. Cook over med heat for around ten mins, sometimes stirring

until its color changes to golden brown & softened. Remove it from heat and add the lemon zest & the chives. Top it with salt & pepper.

2. Alternatively, you should roast these in olive oil at 374 degrees (F) oven for about 35 mins. And add seasonings that you'd like.

Four Ingredient Sugar-Free Cranberry Sauce

(Ready in about 20 mins |Serving 8| Difficulty: Easy)

Per serving: Kcal 21, Fat:0g, Net Carbs:5g Protein:0g

Ingredients

- Bag of cranberries 12 oz

- Water 4 oz

- Trim healthy mama sweet 1 cup

- Vanilla 1 tsp

- Cinnamon 1 tsp

Instructions

1. Stir the cranberries as well as the water in a big saucepan. Cook for around 5 to 7 mins over med heat, until all the berries appear. Bring the rest of the ingredients together & lower the heat to med. Cook until needed fire. Might thicken further as it cools.
2. Put it in the freezer for about 2 weeks.

Pico de Gallo

(Ready in about 15 mins |Serving 6| Difficulty: Easy)

Per serving: Kcal 21, Net Carbs:6g Protein:1g

Ingredients

- Medium tomatoes 6

- Large onion 1

- Fresh cilantro leaves 1 cup

- Lime juice

- Salt

Instructions

1. Cut tomatoes, onion & cilantro into bits. Apply to a wide bowl, then whisk until mixed.
2. If you would like some fire, finely chop jalapeno and add to the bowl then.
3. Place in lime juice and season with salt.
4. Serve or chill before ready.

Low-Carb Onion Rings

(Ready in about 20 mins |Serving 4| Difficulty: Easy)

Per serving: Cal 175, Fat:16g, Net Carbs:4g Protein:3g

Ingredients

- Large onion 1

- Egg 1

- Coconut flour 2 tbsp

- Grated parmesan cheese 2 tbsp

- Garlic powder 1/8 tsp

- Parsley flakes 1/4 tsp

- Cayenne pepper 1/8 tsp

- Taste-salt

- Olive oil to fry 1/4 cup

Instructions

1. Heat the oil in a med pan.
2. In a small cup, smash the egg. In a small dish, mix the coconut flour with parmesan, garlic powder, parsley dust, cayenne, and spice.
3. Cut up the onion to around 1/2 to 3/4-inch-thick & split the rings, so you have a wide bunch. Apply all the onion rings to the egg mixture and completely blend so that they are fully covered. Drench the ointments in the egg for one minute, then move into the coating and then into the hot oil in small batches.
4. Fry until its color changes to a golden brown, then switch to brown the other side with a fork/tongs. To soak up some extra oil, drop to a plate lined with paper towels.
5. Serve with your favorite sauce (sugar-free).

Roasted Spicy Garlic Eggplant Slices

(Ready in about 30 mins |Serving 6| Difficulty: Easy)

Per serving: Kcal 64, Fat:5g, Net Carbs:5g Protein:1g

Ingredients

- Plant egg 1

- Olive oil 2 tbsp

- Garlic powder 1 tsp

- Red pepper 1/2 tsp

- Italian seasoning 1/2 tsp

- Salt 1 tsp

Instructions

1. Heat the oven to 425F.
2. Line a cookie sheet with a bakery release paper.
3. Cut the Aubergine into circles.
4. Place Aubergine slices in a single layer onto a cookie sheet.
5. Put olive oil on both sides of the Aubergine slices.
6. Sprinkle it with garlic powder, red pepper, sweet paprika & Italian seasoning on the Aubergine strips.
7. Place the aubergine in the oven & roast for 25 mins.
8. Aubergine extract from the oven and season with salt.

Roasted Baby Eggplant

(Ready in about 50 mins | Serving 16| Difficulty: Easy)

Per serving: Cal 44, Fat:4g, Net Carbs:1g Protein:1g

Ingredients

- Baby eggplant 1

- Olive oil 2 tbsp

- Kosher 1 tsp

- Ground pepper 1 tsp

- To serve:

- Ricotta cheese 1/3 cup

- Additional virgin olive oil 2 tbsp

- Ground pepper fresh

- Kosher to taste

Instructions

1. Clean the aubergine & slice it up. Place side up on a cutting baking sheet. Add the olive oil & season with fennel pollen, salt & pepper.
2. Bake for about forty-five mins in the 349 degrees (F) oven, or until softened & browned. Take away from the oven & let it cool. Serve warm.
3. Just before having to serve, top with roughly one tsp of cheese of ricotta for each half. Sprinkle with newly crushed peppercorns & just some grains of salt. Drizzle with olive oil of very good quality.

Crispy Fried Eggplant Rounds With Parmesan Cheese and Marinara Sauce

(Ready in about 30 mins |Serving 4| Difficulty: Easy)

Per serving: Kcal 233, Fat:17.26g, Net Carbs:7.15g Protein:11.38g

Ingredients

- Eggplant 1 pound

- Crushed pork rinds 1 cup

- Grated parmesan cheese 1/2 cup

- Dried oregano 1 tsp

- Dried basil 1 tsp

- Salt 1/2 tsp

- Granulated garlic 1/4 tsp

- Onion Powder 1/4 tsp

- Pepper 1/4 tsp

- Beaten large eggs 2

- Olive oil 2 tbsp

Instructions

1. Prep: cut the aubergine into 10 to 12 rings, season with salt & place in such a colander for 15 mins to drain. Fully dry on tissue paper. In the meantime, in a small bowl, beat the eggs, big enough to hold an aubergine round & rush with a fork. In some other small bowl, whisk the pork rinds, cheese & season together. A tiny sheet of pan ready.

2. Procedure: Take around with the fork, then turn it back & forth into the egg until fully covered. Take a fork, then let the egg run away. Place the mixture into the breadcrumbs & cover with crumbs on top. Push the breadcrumbs upwards. Then turn the fork over the row and do it again. Round out the aubergine as well as a mix of the excess breadcrumbs. Lay it down on the sheet pan.

Repeat on all rounds of the procedure. Depending on how large they are, you should have plenty for 10 to 12 rounds.

3. Cook: Heat an iron pan over med-high heat. Alternatively, you can use a large pancake pan and fit everything on your pan at once. Once hot, add the oil. Add 3 to 4 round to your pan once the oil is hot, & now cook for three mins per side. Drain to a towel and then drain to a wire rack. You may have to put more oil to the pan as you go or just lower the heat a bit. The aubergine will be quite crispy & brown.

Artichoke with Herbed Mayonnaise

(Ready in about 40 mins |Serving 4| Difficulty: Easy)

Per Serving: kcal 245; protein 4.1g DV; carbs 12.5g fat 20.9g

Ingredients

- Artichokes 4

- Egg Yolks 2

- Dijon Mustard 1 Tsp

- Lemon Juice 4 Tsp

- Vegetable Oil 1 Cup

- Tarragon 1/4 Cup

- Salt

- Pepper

- Water

Instructions

1. Start by cutting the artichokes' outer leaves with scissors and separating the tops. Use a sharp knife to peel the stem's outer surface, as well as the artichoke's underside.
2. Carry a kettle of water to a boil and put the artichokes in such a steamer. Cook for around twenty mins, or until tender.
3. Have the mayonnaise, whereas the artichokes boil. Stir the egg yolks, vinegar, and lemon juice together. Apply a vegetable oil, then drizzle it slowly into combination while whisking hard. Thoroughly mix until the combination emulsifies & starts thickening. As desired, thin with water, then top with salt & pepper. Apply 1/4 tablespoon of newly herbs to top.
4. When steaming is finished, slice in half the artichokes and extract its choke with a blade.
5. Now happy to eat the artichokes. Eat by peeling off the leaf, dipping in the mayo, and scraping the teeth from the artichoke skin.

Spicy Stir-Fried Sugar Snap Peas

(Ready in about 25 mins |Serving 4| Difficulty: Easy)

Per serving: Cal 93, Fat:3.7g, Net Carbs:8.7g Protein:4.4g

Ingredients

- Sugar snap peas 1 lb.

- Soy sauce 2 t

- Sesame oil 1 tsp

- Sriracha sauce 1 tsp

- Fresh ginger root 3 slices

- Sliced garlic cloves 2 large

- Peanut oil 1 t

Instructions

1. By breaking the stem end & dragging its string down the foot, cut the ties from the sugars (glucose snap pea, then slice individual 1 on the diagonal.
2. Whisk the soy sauce/Soy Sauce Gluten-Free, sesame oil, as well as the Sriracha Sauce.
3. Place the wok on the grill/large frying pan, & preheat for 1 min.
4. Apply the oil once the wok is warm and let it run until the oil shines (approximately 15 to 30 sec depends on how warm the stove gets).
5. Apply the cut root & garlic ginger, then stir-fry only long enough to make them fragrant, add the oil, and cut.
6. Connect the cut sugar snap peas, then cook at high temperature, continuously stirring until the peas become bright green & then just start frying, around 2 mins.
7. Put within sauce combination & simmer for around 2 mins more, stirring continuously, before the sauce begins to cover the peas.
8. If desired, serve sweet, topped with Dark Sesame Seeds

Roasted Cabbage Wedges with Onion Dijon Sauce

(Ready in about 25 mins |Serving 4| Difficulty: Easy)

Per serving: Kcal 140, Fat:12.4g, Net Carbs:7.4g Protein:1.8g

Ingredients

- Green cabbage 1/2 medium about 1½ pounds

- Garlic-infused olive-oil 1 tbsp

- Pepper & salt

Sauce:

- Butter 3 tbsp

- Chopped fresh onion 2 tablespoons

- Dijon mustard 1 tbsp

- Chopped garlic 1/2 tsp

- Each salt & pepper 1/8 tsp

Instructions

1. Preheat oven to 425 ° C. Line a cookie sheet with bakery release paper.
2. Split half of the cabbage into 4 equal slices & put on a ready cookie sheet. Using a pastry brush to cover each wedge's cut side with oil and top with salt pepper. Switch curtains & repeat.
3. In the oven, place the cookie sheet & cook for 10 to 12 mins. Turn the wedges & bake for another 8 to 10 mins more until it's browned.
4. In the meanwhile, apply together with all sauce ingredients to the tiny saucepan and simmer on med heat until the butter is thoroughly melted. Keep it warm.
5. Put the wedges on the tray to eat, mix sauce again, then chop over the wedges. Top it with parsley, or chives, if needed.

Roasted Salt & Pepper Radish Chips

(Ready in about 25 mins |Serving 4| Difficulty: Easy)

Per serving: Kcal 70, Fat:7.1g, Net Carbs:2.2g Protein:0.4g

Ingredients

- Fresh radishes 16 ounce
- Coconut oil melted 2 tbsp
- Sea salt 1/2 tsp
- Pepper 1/2 tsp

Instructions

1. Oven preheated to 400 F.
2. Slice the radishes thinly.
3. Coat with oil.
4. Between 2 cookie sheets, spread radishes do not even overlap.
5. Then mix salt & pepper as well as scatter over the pieces.
6. Cook 12 to 15 mins.

Baked Artichoke Hearts Au Gratin

(Ready in about 1hour 10 mins |Serving 4| Difficulty: Easy)

Per serving: Cal 295, Fat:24g, Net Carbs:15g Protein:9g

Ingredients

- Frozen artichoke hearts one 12 oz, drained, thawed & larger cut in half

- Thinly sliced green onions 1/4 cup

- Olive oil 2 tsp

- Fresh & salty ground black pepper for taste

- Almond flour 1/4 cup

- Parmesan cheese 1/3 cup

- Pecorino Romano cheese 1/3 cup

- Dried thyme 1/2 tsp

- Dried oregano 1/4 tsp

- Mayo 1/3 cup

- Lemon zest 1 tsp

- Lemon juice 2 t

- Garlic puree 1/2 tsp

Instructions

1. Oven preheated to 324F/170 C.
2. If they're already frozen, thaw artichoke hearts in your oven and drain well.
3. Slice bigger artichoke heart in half lengthwise because it's the same size all around.
4. To grease 2 tiny gratin dishes/one med size baking dish, use olive oil.
5. Arrange a single sheet of artichoke hearts in the oiled bowl.
6. Then scatter on the artichokes with thinly chopped green onions, then top with salt & fresh black pepper.

7. Add the almond meal/flour, the Parmesan grated cheese, the pancetta-Romano grated cheese & the herbs.
8. Stir your mayo, lemon juice, lemon zest & garlic puree together, then blend into 1/2 cup cheese combination.
9. Using a rubber scraper to distribute it over the upper end of the artichoke core and set aside the remaining of the crumb or cheese bread combination.
10. Wrap the plates with paper, then bake 30 mins in a 324F/169C oven.
11. Take it from the oven and raise heat to 374F/190C.
12. Lift foil & top the leftover cheese combination.
13. Return to the oven & bake for around 25 mins or until the surface is mildly browned and the plate is hot clear.
14. Serve mild or hot.

Oven Roasted Basil Parmesan Tomatoes

(Ready in about 25 mins |Serving 6| Difficulty: Easy)

Per serving: Cal 60, Fat:2.67g, Net Carbs:4.3g

Ingredients

- Tomatoes 4

- Sea salt 1/2 tsp

- Garlic powder 1/2 tsp

- Onion Powder 1/2 tsp

- Dried oregano 1/2 tsp

- Black pepper 1/4 tsp

- Fresh small basil leaves 12

- Ground parmesan cheese 1/2 cup

Instructions

1. Oven preheated to 425 ° C. Line a rimmed cookie sheet with bakery release paper.
2. Cut the end of the tomatoes, then cut to thirds. If you choose a tomato that is bigger than a Roma, you are expected to get twice the number of slices.
3. Mix the salt, garlic powder, onion powder, oregano, & pepper in a shallow cup.
4. Place the slices of tomatoes over the bakery release paper in such a single layer. Sprinkle with seasoning blend both on sides of every slice.
5. Cover every slice of tomato with the basil leaf, & generously top every slice of grated parmesan.
6. Bake 15 to 20 mins once the cheese becomes golden brown & melted.

Mashed Cauliflower with Parmesan & Chives

(Ready in about 20 mins:| Serving 4-6 | Difficulty: Easy)

Per serving: Kcal 33 Fat 2g Carbs 1g Protein 3g

Ingredients

- Heads cauliflower cored 2 small & leaves removed & cut into small florets

- Chicken broth 2 cups

- Grated parmesan cheese 1/4 cup

- Fresh chopped chives 1/4 cup

- Ground black pepper & kosher salt

Instructions

1. Mix both cauliflower & chicken bouillon in a med saucepan & carry to a simmer.
2. Lower the heat to boil, cover it with a lid, then cook for 15-20 mins or when the cauliflower is soft but does not fall apart entirely.
3. Use a spoon with a slot to move the cauliflower to the mixing bowl and puree until smooth & silky.
4. Move to a dish, season with flake salt & ground black pepper, then mix in the Parmesan & minced chives. Serve hot.

Garlic Mashed Cauliflower

(Ready in about 22 mins :| Serving 4 | Difficulty: Easy)

Per serving: Kcal 101, Fat:9g, Net Carbs:3g Protein:2g

Ingredients

- Large cauliflower 1 divided in small florets

- Cream cheese low fat 3 ounces

- Salted butter 2 tbsp

- Minced garlic sautéed 1 1/2 teaspoon

Instructions

1. Carry a med kettle of water to simmer. The cauliflower is heated for eight to ten mins until it is cooked, or until the pork is soft. Remove cauliflower and wash.

2. Put cauliflower in a blender/food processor together with other ingredients, & pulse until smooth & fluffy.

Goat Cheese Cauliflower Bake Recipe

(Ready in about 30 mins :| Serving 8 | Difficulty: Easy)

Per serving: Cal 226, Fat:13g

Ingredients

- Large Cauliflowers 2 & chopped in 8 cups

- Hickory Smoked Bacon 4 strips

- Onion 1 cup

- Minced Garlic 4 tbsp

- Chopped Goat Cheese 10 ounces

- Low Fat softened Cream Cheese 1/4 cup

- Pepper & Salt to taste

- Sliced Green Onion for garnish

Instructions

1. Oven preheated to 400 ° F then spray the baking spray with a casserole bowl.

2. For 8 mins put the sliced cauliflower in a big bowl & microwave. Mix & microwave again for 8 mins before the fork-tender.

3. Heat a small skillet on med heat as cauliflower cooks, then cook the bacon until its color changes to a golden brown, around 2 to 3 mins on either side. Blotting the extra fat with a clean towel until fried, break it into tiny pieces and put aside. Make sure the bacon fat is stored inside the pan.

4. In med/high pressure, heat the reserved bacon fat & fry both onion & garlic until their color changes to golden brown and tender, only 2 to 3 mins.

5. Move the cooked cauliflower to a big mixing bowl, then substitute your cream cheese & the fried onions in 8 oz of chèvre. Run until well blended & nearly entirely smooth, with a few bits remaining in for texture.

6. Move the cauliflower combination to a med bowl and mix in the diced bacon, then blend until spread uniformly. Sprinkle with salt & pepper.
7. Top with cauliflower in the ready casserole bowl & crumble over the leftover chèvre.
8. Bake for about twenty mins before the top only starts to shine. Decorate it then with green onions & serve.

Cauliflower Cheesy Alla Vodka Casserole

(Ready in about 50 mins :| Serving 1 | Difficulty: Easy)

Per serving: kcal 214, Fat:14g, Net Carbs:6g Protein:12g

Ingredients

- Well-drained cooked cauliflower florets 8 cups

- Vodka sauce 2 cups

- Whipping cream heavy 2 tbsp

- Butter melted 2 tbsp

- Parmesan cheese 1/3 cup

- Kosher salt 1/2 tsp

- Ground pepper black ¼ tsp

- Provolone cheese 6 slices

- Chopped fresh basil 1/4 cup

Instructions

1. In a big bowl, mix the cauliflower, vodka sauce, strong whipping cream, sugar, Parmesan cheese, flake salt, & black pepper, then mix well.
2. Move to a 9 * 13 Casserole & fill with pieces of Provolone/mozzarella cheese.
3. Bake for 30 to 40 minutes in a hot oven 373 degrees (F) or when the baking dish is simmering & the cheese is melted fully.
4. Take it from the oven and leave for around 10 minutes.
5. Now top it with sliced new basil.

Feta Stuffing and Low-Carb Pumpkin Bread

(Ready in about 45 mins :| Serving 10 | Difficulty: Easy)

Per serving: Cal 288, Fat:25g, Net Carbs:3.5g Protein:11g

Ingredients

- Pumpkin bread cubed 4 cups

- Sage flavored pork sausage roll 16 oz

- Chopped onion 1/2 cup

- Chicken 1/3 cup

- Butter 2 tbsp

- Seasoning bell 1 tsp

- Feta cheese crumbled 3/4 cup

- Chopped fresh parsley 2 tbsp

Instructions

1. Toast cubes of pumpkin bread in a preheated oven of 350 degrees (F) for 8 to 10 mins or until its color changes to a golden brown.

2. Fry both sausage & onions together in a med sauté pan until the onions are tender, and the sausage is completely fried.

3. Squeeze 1/4 of a liquid out of a saucepan.

4. Apply the butter, broth & seasoning of Bell, then carry it to boil.

5. Remove it from fire and whisk gently in the cubes of bread, feta & parsley.

6. Move to the baking dish & bake for twenty mins at 375 ° (F) or when the surface becomes golden brown & mildly crunchy.

7. Bake it for 1 hour & serve hot.

Keto Spicy Sausage and Cheddar Stuffing

(Ready in about 3hour 20 mins :| Serving 16 | Difficulty: Easy)

Per serving: Kcal 311, Fat:26.4g, Net Carbs:6g Protein:11.5g

Ingredients

- Cheesy skillet bread 1

- Italian sausage spicy 12 ounces

- Diced celery 1 cup

- Diced onion 1/2 cup

- Minced garlic cloves 2

- Dried sage 1 tsp

- Kosher salt 1/2 tsp

- Black pepper 1/4 tsp

- Chicken broth low sodium 1/2 cup

- large eggs 2

- heavy cream 1/4 cup

Instructions

1. Create the skillet bread & cut into 1/2-inch bits, one day/two in advance. The oven preheated to the 200F.
2. Place the cubes of bread over a wide baking sheet and bake for two to three hrs., until it's dried and crisp. Let them hang out overnight to carry on drying.
3. Heat a large pan on med heat & include sausage; sauté with a wooden spoon only until cooked through, around six mins, breaking up big pieces.
4. Move sausage to the wide bowl, using a spoon with a slot. Apply celery, onion, garlic, basil, salt &

pepper to pan, then sauté for around five mins, until tender. Decorate with bacon.

5. Oven Preheat to 350F, and a big glass. Casserole measuring 13 x 9 inch with butter. Substitute sausage combination of cubed crust. Add the broth and mix the chicken to blend.

6. Stir eggs with milk in a med dish, then spill the mixture into a bowl. Toss and move it to ready Casserole until well mixed. Bake uncovered for 35 mins until the surface is browned & crusty.

Gluten-Free Stuffing & Low-Carb

(Ready in about 18 mins |Serving 1 | Difficulty: Easy)

Per serving: Cal 203, Fat:16g, Net Carbs:4g Protein:8g

Ingredients

- Mild sausage rolls 12 oz

- Chopped onion 1/2 cup

- Chopped celery 1 cup

- Chopped cauliflower1 head

- White wine 1/2 cup

- Chopped walnuts 1/4 cup

- Chopped parsley 1/4 cup

- Minced fresh sage 1 tsp

- Pepper & salt to taste

Instructions

1. Fry your sausage in such a big sauté skillet & cut it into tiny bits. Apply your onions & celery to a saucepan and simmer for 5 mins or until softened.

2. Apply the cauliflower & simmer for about eight minutes. You want to keep it a little darker & caramelize, so don't mix very much. Apply the white wine & boil over med heat until there is no liquid left only at the bottom of a skillet.

3. Add on the walnuts & then fry for 2 minutes. Remove it from fire, and whisk in the sage and parsley. Season it with salt & pepper.

Low-Carb Tortillas

(Ready in about 20 mins |Serving 16 | Difficulty: Easy)

Per serving: Kcal 50, Fat:1.5g, Net Carbs:2.75g
Protein:8.5g

Ingredients

- Large Eggs 8

- Coconut flour 1/3 cup

- Water 10 tbsp

- Baking powder 1/4 tsp

- Garlic powder 1/4 tsp

- Onion Powder 1/4 tsp

- Chili powder 1/4 tsp

- Pink Salt 1/4 tsp

Instructions

1. In a cup, apply the egg, coconut powder, baking soda & water. Mix well (the combination must be standardized and watery).

2. Warm the skillet on lower heat. Wait until the skillet is heated, spray with a baking spray & fall a few of the combination into the middle.

3. Tilt the pan on both corners asap and scatter your batter as evenly as possible.

4. Cook it before it begins to rise or bubble for a few minutes until you pick it up & the different side had browned. Turn & cook for one minute.

5. Repeat until the batter is all fried. For us, the mixture above rendered 16 little taco-sized tortillas.

6. TIP: If the first tortilla might not lay evenly enough on the pan, apply additional water to the white egg mixture and blend it.

Two Mins Low-Carb English Muffin

(Ready in about 4 mins |Serving 2 | Difficulty: Easy)

Per serving: Kcal 222, Fat:20g, Net Carbs:3g Protein:7g

Ingredients

- Unsweetened almond butter cashew 2 tbsp

- Butter 1 tbsp

- Almond flour 2 tbsp

- Salt 1/8 tsp

- Baking powder 1/2 tsp

- Almond milk unsweetened 1 tbsp

- The egg has beaten 1

Instructions

1. Sprinkle with olive oil baking spray/coconut oil spray your ramekin.
2. Apply butter & almond butter to the platter.
3. For thirty-sec microwave, then blend it until smooth. Put aside to chill.
4. Whisk together almond meal/flour, cinnamon, & baking soda/powder in a tiny bowl.
5. To dry products, add the milk & the egg and mix until combined.
6. Place this mixture over almond butter combination into a small ramekin and whisk to mix properly.
7. Microwave it for two mins.
8. Let chill it for a few mins before extracting it from the ramekin & cutting in half toast.
9. Toast if you like.

Cheesy Garlic Bread Muffins

(Ready in about 45 mins |Serving 12 | Difficulty: Easy)

Per serving: Kcal 322, Fat:27.17g, Net Carbs:7.44g Protein:12.83g

Ingredients

- Melted butter 6 tbsp

- Garlic pressed 5 cloves

- Sour cream 1/2 cup

- Large eggs 4

- Salt 1 tsp

- Almond flour 3 cups

- Baking powder 2 tsp

- Cheddar cheese shredded 1 cup

- Chopped parsley 1/4 cup

- Shredded mozzarella 4 ounces

- Salt for taste

Instructions

1. Oven preheated to 325F, and well grease a regular nonstick muffin pan. Place muffin pan on the wide-rimmed cookie sheet.
2. Mix softened butter & garlic cloves 3.
3. Mix your sour cream, eggs, leftover garlic, & salt in a high-speed blender/food processor. Mixed phase as well. Apply the almond flour/meal, baking powder, bacon, & parsley then begin to cook until smooth.
4. Split halves of batter b/w the ready muffin cups& create a tiny well in the middle of each using a spoon.
5. Split the sliced mozzarella b/w the muffins and push into wells. Sprinkle with such a combination of about 1 teaspoon of garlic butter.
6. Split the leftover batter b/w each cup of muffins, making sure the cheese is coated in the best way

possible. Blend the leftover garlic butter over the tops & sprinkle it with salt.

7. Bake for around 25 mins, until the tops become golden brown as well as solid if touch. They can leak a lot of oil when they bake, and it will leak some over the sides (hence the cookie sheet lower- to save the oven).

8. Remove and allow it to cool for ten mins before serving it to guests. From the oven, they're great and mild only with cheese already gooey. They're cold and heat up quickly too.

Braided Garlic Breadsticks

(Ready in about 35 mins |Serving 8 | Difficulty: Easy)

Per serving: Kcal 229, Fat:18g, Net Carbs:7g Protein:10g

Ingredients

Dough Ingredients:

- Shredded mozzarella 8 oz

- Cream cheese 2 oz

- Egg 1

- Coconut flour 1/3 cup

- Almond flour 1/3 cup

- Golden ground flaxseed 1/3 cup

- Baking powder 2 tsp

Garlic Butter Topping:

- Melted butter 2 tbsp

- Garlic crushed 2 cloves

- Pinch of "salt."

Instructions

1. Oven preheated to 400. Mix both butter & garlic, which is minced. Set Down. Line the baking sheet with parchment.

2. Place cheese in a safe bowl in a microwave oven. 1 min Microwave. Shake. Again, Microwave for thirty sec. Shake. Any cheese will be melting on that stage. Microwave another 30 seconds before uniform & gloopy. Add the ingredients into the egg & dry. You may need to pour it on wax paper, then knead this by hand to mix your ingredients completely, or you may do this with the dough tool of a mixing bowl.

3. Push the bakery release paper into a wide rectangle. Split into 8 lines in a lengthwise direction. Break every strip into three smaller pieces, lengthwise. You're going to end up having twenty-four strips. Apply three strips to roofs. Braid your dough. Connect bottom & tuck under.

Place your braid on the cookie sheet coated with a parchment. Allow producing 8 sticks of braided bread.

4. Clean each of them with garlic butter You need to have some of the small garlic bits on them too. Toss a tiny quantity of salt though on your breadsticks.

5. Cook fifteen Mins to prepare. Remove from heat & coat with the remaining garlic butter. Bake 5 to 10 mins, or its color changes to a golden brown. Serve hot.12. Asiago Zucchini.

Bread and dried Sun Tomato – Low-Carb

(Ready in about 1hour 30 mins |Serving 12| Difficulty: Easy)

Per serving: kcal 262, Fat:23g, Net Carbs:3g Protein:8g

Ingredients

- Salted melted butter 3/4 cup

- Eggs 4

- Almond milk unsweetened 1/2 cup

- Zucchini shredded 1/2 cup, crushed dry in a paper towel

- Dried sun tomatoes chopped 2 tbsp

- Almond flour 2 cups

- Coconut flour 1/4 cup

- Baking powder 4 tsp

- Granulated sugar 1 tsp

- Xanthan gum 1/2 tsp

- Kosher salt 1 1/4 tsp

- Dried oregano 1/2 tsp

- Dried parsley 1/2 tsp

- Garlic powder 1/4 tsp

- Ground asiago cheese 1/2 cup

Instructions

1. Oven Preheated to 350 ° C (F)
2. In a grinder, mix (wet ingredients) together with all the butter, peas, almond milk, zucchini & dried tomatoes, then blend for around thirty seconds or almost smooth.
3. Blend all the (dry ingredients) coconut flour, almond flour, baking soda, sweetener, xanthan gum, cinnamon, oregano, parsley, garlic powder in the med sized bowl and combine with a fork until well mixed without lumps.

4. place the dry ingredients into the wet ingredients and combine with a fork until it creates a smooth batter and absorbs the dry ingredients.
5. Mix in cheese made in Asiago.
6. In a greased loaf tin/twelve muffin cups, spoon your batter.
7. Bake for 1 hr. at 350 ° (F) while creating a loaf.
8. When creating muffins, bake at 350 ° (F) for twenty to twenty-five mins.

Low-Carb Cranberry Relish (Keto)

(Ready in about 15 mins |Serving 12| Difficulty: Easy)

Per serving: Kcal 17, Fat:24g, Net Carbs:4g

Ingredients

- Ocean fresh Spray cranberries 12 ounces

- 4 oz orange 1 med

- Swerve Granulated 2/3 cup

- Fresh ginger juice 1 tsp

- Ground cloves 3 pinches

Instructions

1. Clean your cranberries & remove any weak berries or tiny stones. Slice the stem & the end of Florida State Flower to the skin, then segment it & break in half per slice. Don't take off the orange. Throw out the seeds. Chop a slice of ginger approximately

84

1 inch. In a coffee/spice grinder, pulverize the sweetener.

2. In the blender lie both cranberries as well as orange bits and apply the sweetener, cinnamon & juice of ginger.

3. In the food processor, blend both the cranberries & orange until they are chopped into approximately the same sized bits. If you like it to be sweeter, apply your preferred stevia sweetener/more crushed Sukrin

4. Refrigerate for up to 2 days until use, usually for 5-7 days. Makes about three cups each serving, plus 1/4 cup.

Parmesan Garlic Roasted Mushrooms

(Ready in about 30 mins |Serving 8| Difficulty: Easy)

Per serving: Cal 151, Fat:14g, Net Carbs:5g Protein:2g

Ingredients

- Cleaned & trimmed mushrooms 1 pound
- Chopped large cloves garlic 3
- Olive oil 2 tbsp
- Minced olives 2 tbsp
- Fresh lemon juice 2 tsp
- Chopped flat-leaf 1/4 c
- Pepper & salt to taste
- Butter 3 tbsp
- Shredded parmesan cheese 1/4 c fresh

Instructions

1. Oven Preheated to 450 degrees and gently spray nonstick oil on a small baking dish. Toss with mushrooms, oil, garlic, olives and capers, lemon juice, salt, parsley, & pepper together in your bowl. Dot the butter uniformly on the upper edge of mushrooms, then roast through the baking process for twenty mins, turning halfway.

2. Take it from your oven, turn that broiler on and cover the oven shelf. Toss the cheese over mushrooms, then move to the oven on top broil & rack before the cheese is melted and start browning for around 3 mins.

Creamy Cauliflower Mash with Kale (Low-Carb Colcannon)

(Ready in about 30 mins |Serving 4| Difficulty: Easy)

Per serving: Kcal 112, Fat:5g, Net Carbs:16g Protein:6g

Ingredients

- One large head cauliflower (6 cups) trim up in florets

- Unsalted butter 4 tsp

- Chopped kale 3 cups

- Crushed garlic 4 cloves

- Minced scallions 2

- Free fat milk 1/3 cup

- Pepper & kosher salt

Instructions

1. Simmer the cauliflower: Place the cauliflower in such a med pot and cover one inch with cold water. Apply salt, then bring it to a boil.
2. Cook, tender before the fork. Six to eight mins. Drain it through a colander (reserve any liquid if necessary).
3. Melt 1 tsp of med-high heat butter in the same pot. Apply the garlic & green onions, fry thirty sec, add the leaf cabbage, 1/4 teaspoon salt, cover & cook until wilted, 6-7 mins.
4. Puree your cauliflower w milk in a processor, move the greens to the pot and apply 1/2 tsp butter, 1/4 tsp salt & pepper.
5. Put it in a bowl and season with leftover tsp butter to eat.

Parmesan Rosti & Low-Carb Celeriac Bacon

(Ready in about 10 mins |Serving 2| Difficulty: Easy)

Per serving: Cal 137, Fat:15g, Net Carbs:4g Protein:5g

Ingredients

- Raw minced bacon, 2 Tbsp

- Butter 1 Tbsp

- Olive oil 2 tsp

- Shredded raw Celeriac 1 cup

- Minced fresh parsley 1 tsp

- Grated Parmesan cheese 2 Tbsp

- Flake salt 1/2 tsp

- Ground black pepper 1/8 tsp

- Garlic powder 1/4 tsp

Instructions

1. Cook your bacon within the olive oil & butter in 12 to 14 inches sauté skillet, until almost all become crispy. In the meanwhile, add and blend well the chopped celeriac, parsley, grated parmesan cheese, salt, pepper & garlic powder. Apply the celeriac combination to the saucepan, then blend well with the fried bacon. Push the mixture onto the hot pan with a broad spoon at the back to create a circular shape.

2. Cook for around five mins at low-med heat, or until its color changes to golden brown (dark) and crispy on the sides & soften the rest. Place the serving platter carefully over the pan and turn the cake crisply side up onto it. Serve warm, decorated with additional parsley If needed.

Garlic Butter Sautéed Spinach

(Ready in about 8 mins |Serving 2| Difficulty: Easy)

Per serving: Cal 71, Fat:4.6g, Net Carbs:4g Protein:3.7g

Ingredients

- Salted melted butter 2 tbsp

- 4 cloves garlic minced

- Baby spinach 8 oz

- Salt 1 pinch

- Lemon juice 1 tsp

Instructions

1. Warm a pan up, then apply the butter. Sauté your garlic until aromatic, apply the spinach to the pan, then incorporate the salt & lemon juice and mix well to blend.
2. Remove from the heat and switch to a serving plate until spinach leaves begin to wilt.
3. Garnish with new slices of lemon and serve right away.

Low-Carb Coconut Creamed Spinach

(Ready in about 4 mins |Serving 1| Difficulty: Easy)

Per serving: Cal 73, Fat:7g, Net Carbs:1g Protein:2g

Ingredients

- Coconut milk 1/4 cup

- Baby spinach 4 cups

- Nutmeg 1/8 tsp

- Granulated sugar 2 tsp

- Cayenne pepper 1/8 tsp

- Salt to taste

Instructions

1. Heat coconut milk for around two mins in a shallow sauté pan. Apply the leaves of spinach and mix until wilted, bright green. Add seasonings, try & adjust when appropriate.
2. Serve it.

Buttery Bacon Brussels Sprouts

(Ready in about 20 mins |Serving 5| Difficulty: Easy)

Per serving: Kcal 120, Fat:10g, Net Carbs:3.8g Protein:3g

Ingredients

- Brussels sprouts 400 g

- Bacon 2 slices

- Butter 55 g

- Crushed garlic 1/2 clove

- Walnuts 4 pieces

Instructions

1. Prepare the sprouts in Brussels by eliminating every dirty leaf, slightly trim the root, and split in half.
2. Simmer in a limited volume of water, about 5 to 8 mins until fully done. Drain and keep the lid off to make the steam run. You wouldn't want a soggy sauce.
3. Heat the butter in a pan and fry the bacon softly before it starts to go crispy. Now apply the garlic and proceed to fry for one minute. Be alert not to make the garlic burnt.
4. Then apply the zest of orange and whisk gently in the sprouts cooked in Brussels. Mix in the buttery garlic sauce when heating the Brussels sprouts to coat them.
5. Serve & use a few bits of walnut for garnish.

Stir-Fried Bok Choy with Soy Butter & Sauce

(Ready in about 15 mins |Serving 4| Difficulty: Easy)

Per serving: Cal 119, Fat:11g, Net Carbs:4g Protein:3g

Ingredients

- Water 2 t

- soy sauce 2 tsp

- sesame oil 1 tsp

- oyster sauce 1 t

- vegetable oil 1 t

- trimmed heads bok choy 2 & cut crosswise in strips

- salt 1/2 tsp

- butter 1 t

Instructions

1. Mix all the water, soy sauce, sesame seed, as well as the oyster sauce.

2. Though until hot, around 1 to 2 mins, heat wok/frying pan, Now add oil & cook for around thirty sec.

3. Apply salt, then bok choy, & stir-fry for two minutes.

4. Apply a combination of soy sauce & butter, then fry for another 1 to 2 mins until bok choy is somewhat crispy but becomes soft.

5. Serve warm, if needed, seasoned with sesame oil.

Low-Carb Cheesy Brussels Sprouts Gratin

(Ready in about 40 mins |Serving 8| Difficulty: Easy)

Per serving: Kcal 253, Fat:19g, Net Carbs:10g Protein:8g

Ingredients

- Removed Brussels Sprouts stems 2 pounds

- Additional virgin olive oil 2 tbsp

- Salt 1/2 tsp

- Pepper 1/4 tsp

- Heavy cream 1 cup

- White cheddar grated 1 cup

- Zest 1 lemon

- White pepper 1/4 tsp

- Asiago cheese grated 1/3 cup

Instructions

1. Oven Preheated to 400 F.
2. Cut Brussels Sprinkles in two, & mix in a bowl of oil.
3. Season with pepper & salt on a baking tray/cast iron pan.
4. Cook for about twenty mins.
5. Mix heavy whipping cream, cheddar, zest of lemon & pepper together in another dish.
6. Place on the Sprouts in Brussels.
7. Sprinkle over dried Asiago.
8. Cook 10 to 15 mins either hot before it bubbles & steams.
9. If needed, season with parsley (fresh).

Low-Carb Creamy Greek Zucchini Patties

(Ready in about 40 mins |Serving 24| Difficulty: Easy)

Per serving: Cal 53, Fat:5g, Net Carbs:2g Protein:2g

Ingredients

- Zucchini 2 lbs.
- Large organic eggs 2
- Fresh herbs large handfuls 2
- Breadcrumbs 1 cup
- Crumbled feta cheese 1 cup
- Ground cumin 1 tsp
- Fine-grain sea salt 1 tsp
- Ground black pepper
- Olive oil 3 tbsp

Instructions

1. Clean the courgettes, then break its end off. Grate these on grates side gaps.

2. In a colander, put grated courgettes, & season with salt. Let drain for a minimum of ten mins (best 1 hour).

3. Take the courgettes handfuls, then suck out all the moisture. Beat the eggs in a big bowl, add the grated courgettes, basil, cumin, almond meal/flour/, feta, pepper & salt. Okay, blend as properly.

4. Move the mixture to the fridge for 20 mins so that the almond meal will soak up more of the moisture.

5. Take a couple of handfuls of combinations & form them into patties. If it is sticky, apply one tbsp of even more almond meal/flour at a time.

6. Heat a tbsp of olive oil on med-high heat in the big nonstick skillet. When the patties are hot cooked in lots (do not overload them) for around five mins each side, until golden brown.

7. Remove and rinse quickly to catch up with the extra oil on a paper towel.

Spaghetti Squash with Garlic and Parsley

(Ready in about 1hour |Serving 4| Difficulty: Easy)

Per serving: Kcal 89, Fat:6g, Net Carbs:8g Protein:3g

Ingredients

- Spaghetti squash 1 large

- Butter soft 3 tbsp

- Chopped small garlic 2 cloves

- Chopped parsley 2-3 tbsp

- Grated parmesan cheese 1/2 cup

- Pepper & salt to taste

Instructions

1. Oven preheated to 375 & put the rack halfway through. Line a baking pan with bakery release paper.

2. Slice the vegetable spaghetti in half-length and pinch the seeds out. Chop the parsley as well as garlic & put in a tiny bowl. Apply the butter melted, then stir it with a spoon.
3. Rub the butter into the cavity and around the sliced parts of the vegetable spaghetti.
4. Cook for 45 to 60 mins.
5. Let it cool so the squash can be treated and scraped off the surface. In Parmesan cheese, salt & pepper to try and blend.
6. Around 3/4 tassels each meal.

Spaghetti Squash with Garlic, Bacon & Parmesan

(Ready in about 50 mins |Serving 6| Difficulty: Easy)

Per serving: Kcal 113, Fat:6g, Net Carbs:11g Protein:2g

Ingredients

- 4 pounds spaghetti squash 1
- Bacon diced 4 slices
- Chopped garlic 3 cloves
- Parmesan cheese shaved
- Pepper & salt

Instructions

1. Oven preheated to 375 °. Spray the cookie sheet with baking spray.

2. Clean the vegetable spaghetti, then pick the stem off the top. Keep this up with side cut down smooth. Cut the squash lengthwise in two.

3. Scrounge the seeds off the squash center and remove. Sprinkle pepper & salt into the squash.

4. Put it on the ready pan and cook for 30 to 45 mins or with just a little resistance, until a fine knife could be quickly placed.

5. Cook the bacon until crispy, on med heat. Apply the garlic to bacon & bake for 1 min, until it is fragrant.

6. Using a fork to remove lengthy strips of flesh from in the squash. Put it in a bowl.

7. Apply bacon & garlic to the squash bowl.

8. Season with salt & pepper, then brush on certain Parmesan cheese.

THANK YOU

Thank you for choosing *Ketogenic Diet: Side Dishes Cookbook* for improving your cooking skills! I hope you enjoyed the recipes while making them and tasting them! If you're interested in learning new recipes and new meals to cook, go and check out the other books of the serie.